TEN HOUSES

Edited by Oscar Riera Ojeda

Peter L. Gluck and Partners

Rockport Publishers, Inc.
Rockport, Massachusetts

First published in the United States of America by:

Rockport Publishers, Inc.

146 Granite Street

Rockport, Massachusetts 01966-1299

Telephone: (508) 546-9590

Fax: (508) 546-7141

ISBN 1-56496-314-4

10 9 8 7 6 5 4 3 2 1

Cover Photograph: Mies House Pavilions and Second Addition / Photograph by Norman McGrath

Back Cover Images (Left to right from top): Pages 18, 20, 32, 42, 56, 63, 76, 86, 92, 103

Page 2: Bridge House / Photograph by Paul Warchol

Printed in Hong Kong

Graphic Design: Lucas Guerra / Oscar Riera Ojeda

Layout: Oscar Riera Ojeda

Contents

Selected Works

Text by Peter Gluck

Foreword

by Oscar Riera Ojeda

At first glance, this collection of houses might appear to arise from disparate sources and different points of view. Yet it is all the work of a single architect, Peter L. Gluck, who resists the conventional practice of quickly comprehensible and easily recognizable design trademarks. Instead, his confident and distinctive approach—clearly expressed in each of the works represented here—leads to richly creative and specific solutions rather than to the stylistic repetition that often characterizes the recent works of other renowned architects of his generation.

In a world of the sound bite and instant brand-name packaging, the complexity of this calm, determinedly inconsistent work is not to be navigated from the surface alone. One has to enter the labyrinth, follow its apparent incongruities, and comprehend the subtlety and depth of detail as well as the intelligent resolution of real architectural and programmatic demands. Then one sees the strong, common stance that animates projects that are otherwise quite different in their expression.

His buildings succeed because they respond to a series of dialectical oppositions, the most universal of which is the tension between the concrete human experience of the house (its program and use) and the abstract demands of architectural form. In a spirit of architectural inquiry, his work explores the dialectical tensions between East and West, inside and outside, back and front, architecture and sculpture, natural and constructed landscape, and other commonly confronted but not interrogated conditions of building reality.

By analyzing these ten houses as a group—from their vertebral structure to their cellular detail and their craftsman-like construction, we have the luxury of completing the architectural puzzle. We see both his modernist commitment and his determination to liberate and expand upon its principles in a freer and more inclusive manner. In these ten projects, his fervent quest for new—but always integrated—horizons within modernism guided his creative explorations in three directions, defined, in his words, as "masked" modernism, "contextual" modernism, and "bold" (or outright) modernism. The series of three pitched-roofed houses at the beginning of the book are representative of masked modernism; Gluck uses familiar readings of "house," but in integral modernist form. In contextual modernism, exemplified by three additions to existing houses, he respects their context but does not reproduce it, insisting on "multiple readings" of both the old original and the new modernist structures. In the bold modernism of the last four houses, he uses abstract form in ways that demand a singular reading and reveals the possibilities of a new, inclusionary modernism.

This compilation of houses designed by Peter L. Gluck highlights his multifaceted search for solutions, in which architecture is always capable of providing more than one answer.

Bridge House, Olive Bridge, New York

Introduction

by Paul Goldberger

Peter Gluck is a modernist who admires Sir Edwin Lutyens, and that curious fact may be the single most revealing thing about him. It tells us that Gluck is something of an iconoclast—Lutyens, after all, was one of the great classicists Britain has ever produced, hardly the role model you would expect for an American architect whose inclinations lean strongly toward modernism. Lutyens, however, was no by-the-book classicist; his buildings were nimble dances, works of invention far more than works of imitation. Classicism for Lutyens was a language, not an ideology, precisely how Peter Gluck approaches modernism. Gluck delights in imaginative solutions to complex problems, and what unifies his work is not similarity of appearance, but a sense of consistent purpose, of intelligent inquiry, and of pleasure in both the sensual and the cerebral elements of form and space.

There is no standard Peter Gluck building: they look as different as the situations, the sites, and the clients that generate them. Throughout all of his various works, however, there is a crispness to both the physical forms he designs and the philosophy embodied within those forms. Gluck buildings are not soft, and they are not sentimental. Instead, it could be said that Peter Gluck is devoted to achieving with harder edges what other architects do with the more picturesque forms of historicism: to provide a sense of comfort, even of nurture, as well as a profound sense of connection to context. Gluck produces modernist buildings in accord with the post-modern value system that sees the building not as a pure and abstract sculptural object, but as a thing whose physical form is responsive to its surroundings as well as to its program.

It is no accident, then, that more than a few of Gluck's most notable buildings have been additions to existing structures. The older houses have ranged from a Federal-style farmhouse in upstate New York to a Mies van der Rohe–designed villa in suburban Connecticut to a Frank Lloyd Wright–influenced house in a Usonian community in Westchester County, none of which was particularly inviting to expansion—indeed, it would be difficult to imagine buildings more self-contained and complete in themselves. How to expand them without

compromising the integrity of the original? In no instance was Gluck's solution to replicate the architecture of the original building, but his response was significantly different in each case. The Federal farmhouse was expanded with a long, low complex of geometric masses, made of glass, stone, metal, and wood, which together form a precisely balanced composition that manages to be at once assertive and deferential. The new wings for the Mies building were, if anything, an even more delicate problem—Gluck's solution was not counterpoint, as in the farmhouse, but a subtle riff on Miesian form, distinct enough in its details so that no one could mistake it for an attempt to duplicate Mies's architecture, but utterly respectful in its overall sensibility, particularly in its massing. For the Wrightian house, set on a steep hill and designed by a former Wright apprentice, Gluck created a curving stucco base below the original building—a barrel-shaped plinth recalling Wright's fondness for circular forms. Yet the addition is no more literally Wrightian than the Mies addition was literally Miesian: it is responsive to the spirit and sensibility of the original esthetic, not directly imitative of it.

All these houses make clear that Gluck's is an architecture of composition and detail in equal measure. Yet for all of the precision of his work, Gluck also is capable of bold gestures. The two-sided house in Lincoln, Massachusetts, must be the most blatant example of a single building with two completely different facades since James Gamble Rogers put a Gothic face on one side of Davenport College at Yale and a Georgian face on the other. (Did this building subliminally influenced Gluck, a graduate both of Yale University and its architecture school?) Yet comparing Gluck's building to Rogers's is hardly fair, since the Yale building switches styles with a jarring abruptness, whereas Gluck's most notable achievement in this house is the subtle way in which he has affected a gradual transformation. The front facade on the street is an abstracted gable, acknowledging both the architectural context of Lincoln and the owner's desire for privacy. In the rear, facing a landscape of river, lawn, and woods, the house opens up into a two-story, sleek, white modernist composition

But it is the sides that are the most interesting—we see the sides of a sloping roof, intercepted by the front gable; Gluck has in effect woven the two facades together, forcing these two opposing architectural languages into conversation.

Forcing conversations that others might avoid is, in a very real sense, a theme of Peter Gluck's work. The house on Lake Michigan seems at once to pay homage to Wright's second Herbert B. Jacobs House, to the buildings of the International Style, and to a general love of geometric abstraction, here some-how seeming not at all arbitrary. This house's massing makes it somewhat discordant, but Gluck manages to confer upon it a sense of rational purpose rather than architectural whim. The most striking thing about this facet of Peter Gluck's work is the sense we have that this forced conversation is actually getting somewhere.

I have said nothing so far about what may be the most important, if not always the most obvious, influence in Gluck's work—the architecture of Japan, where he lived and worked for several years in the early 1970s. Japanese architecture reveals itself literally in such details as the copper leaders, limestone urns, and teak light fixtures at the entry of his sumptuous Manor House with Music in Westchester County (a house whose gabled facade also bears a striking resem-blance to Lutyens's Barton St. Mary), and the remarkable trusswork of wood in both the Federal farmhouse addition and Gluck's own country house (a renova-ted farmhouse to which have been added a series of abstract outbuildings that comment gently on the nature of family and village). The Japanese influence, however, remains in the background, where it confers a particular sensibility— the enabling sensibility, we might call it, for the coherence Gluck brings out of complex and often contradictory forms. Western architecture is generally serene in proportion to its simplicity: the less going on, the calmer it feels. Japanese architecture, by contrast, is often able to be intensely active at no cost to its serenity. Gluck, somehow, has absorbed this power, and makes it work within an otherwise Western context. His buildings are active, complex, busy— and almost always serene.

Gluck's work contains hints of whimsy, but never so much as to make us want to describe these buildings as witty. His architecture takes itself too seriously for that, but coming close to whimsy without going all the way is, for Gluck, evocative of his glancing allusions to Historicism. He sees what it is about, he understands its purpose, but his main order of business is to do something else. This work comes close to being many other things, but it turns out to be, in the end, very much its own—not about history or context or modernism or tradition or purity of form and space, but about what gets produced when an architect cares about every one of these things, and stakes his claim on their coexistence.

Paul Goldberger is Chief Cultural Correspondent for The New York Times, and has served as architecture critic for the paper since 1973. The author of several books on architecture, including The Skyscraper and On the Rise: Architecture and Design in a Post-Modern Age, he lectures widely on architecture, design, planning, and historic preservation. He won the Pulitzer Prize for his architecture criticism in 1984.

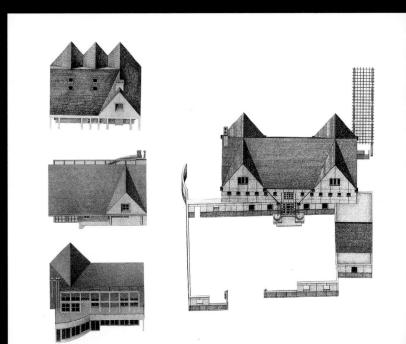

Three-Gable House

Lakeville, Connecticut

M eeting the challenge of building a house of distinction with inexpensive materials and conventional construction, this design packed the largest number of rooms into the least costly shape. A residence of grace and integrity was produced within the constraints of a typical builder's house.

The pitched roof provided the theme. Like the child's drawing of "house" with its single gable, front door, and chimney, the pitched-roof house epitomizes the traditional American idea of home. Long the evocative image of the single-family house, the pitched roof, while comforting and familiar, need not preclude modernist interpretations of sculpture and form. Here the exaggerated pitched roofs do not simply cap the house but are integral to its sculptural shape, both inside and out. Two deeply recessed windows accentuate the exterior mass, and inside, the steep angles enhance the space by utilizing the full volume of the roofs.

The formal organization reflects the classical configuration of base, column, and capital. The first floor, situated partially below grade on the hillside site, acts as the base for the recessed colonnade of the second floor, which supports the pediment of the gabled roofs. In less than five thousand square feet, the house contains a large two-story living room, kitchen, master bedroom suite, four bedrooms, three baths, powder room, laundry room, storage room, and two-car garage.

By limiting the palette to two basic builder's materials—asphalt shingles and acrylic stucco—costs were kept low, and details like the colonnade, which conceals the standard lumberyard windows, give grandeur to the otherwise ordinary program and construction. The house is spacious inside, and viewed from a distance, has sculptural presence far beyond its means.

Above: Retaining walls support bermed earth to create the proverbial suburban driveway-plus-basketball-court. The standard two-car garage door is hidden from the entrance, main level, and lawns, and the usually ad-hoc play space is given formal clarity and architectural definition.

Opposite Page: The three gables, their traditional form expressed as sculptural abstraction, present the house to the country road, the lake view, and the Connecticut hills. The second-floor overhang shields the first-floor windows from the southwest sun, and the colonnade beneath it jumps the scale of the facade, enhancing its formal purity, and also conceals the first floor's inexpensive standard windows and their conventional programmatic placement.

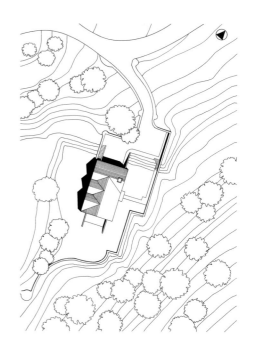

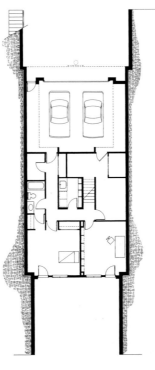

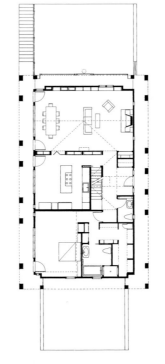

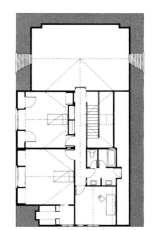

Above: A strong single gable on the north facade marks the formal entrance to the "house"; here, the traditional image is even more abstracted than in the three gables opposite.

Left: The original garage was later converted into a playroom, and a detached garage was built into the hill, its gabled form echoing and complementing the larger composition.

Right: The pitched roofs, chosen for their evocative symbolism and their low cost, also provide the occasion for expressive interior forms and spaces. Here, the typical double-loaded, second-floor hallway breaks through to the two-story, peaked living room.

Opposite Page: Ordinary residential elements—such as stairways and bookshelves—become opportunities for sculptural expression and for the play of light and mass.

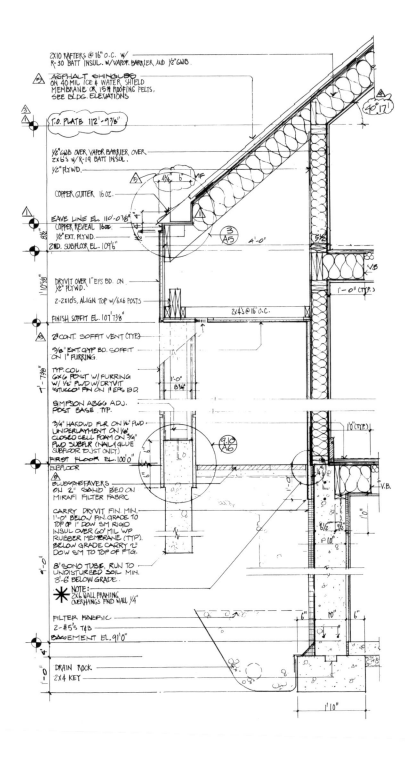

2x10 RAFTERS @ 16" O.C. W/
R-30 BATT INSUL. W/VAPOR. BARRIER, AND 1/2"GWB.

ASPHALT SHINGLES
ON 40 MIL ICE & WATER SHIELD
MEMBRANE OR 15# ROOFING FELTS,
SEE BLDG. ELEVATIONS

T.O. PLATE 112'-9 7/8"

1/2"GWB OVER VAPOR BARRIER OVER
2x6's W/R-19 BATT INSUL.
1/2" PLYWD.

COPPER GUTTER 16 OZ.

EAVE LINE EL. 110'-0 7/8"
COPPER REVEAL 16oz.
1/2" EXT. PLYWD.
2ND. SUBFLOOR EL. 109'6"

DRYVIT OVER 1" EPS BD. ON
1/2" PLYWD.
2-2x10's, ALIGN TOP W/6x6 POSTS

2x4's @ 16' O.C.

FINISH SOFFIT EL. 107' 7 3/8"

2" CONT. SOFFIT VENT (TYP.)

5/8" EXT. GYP. BD. SOFFIT
ON 1" FURRING.

TYP. COL.
6x6 POST W/ FURRING
W/ 1/2" PLYWD W/DRYVIT
"STUCCO" FIN ON 1" EPS BD.

SIMPSON AB66 ADJ.
POST BASE, TYP.

3/4" HARDWD FLR ON 1/2" PLYWD.
UNDERLAYMENT ON 1/8"
CLOSED CELL FOAM ON 3/4"
PLYWD SUBFLR (NAIL & GLUE
SUBFLOOR TO JST ONLY)

FIRST FLOOR EL. 100'0"
SUBFLOOR

BLUESTONE PAVERS
ON 2" SAND BED ON
MIRAFI FILTER FABRIC

CARRY DRYVIT FIN. MIN.
1'-0" BELOW FIN. GRADE TO
TOP OF 1" DOW SM RIGID
INSUL OVER 60 MIL WP
RUBBER MEMBRANE (TYP).
BELOW GRADE CARRY 2"
DOW SM TO TOP OF FTG.

8" SONO TUBE, RUN TO
UNDISTURBED SOIL MIN.
3'-6 BELOW GRADE.

* NOTE:
2x6 WALL FRAMING
OVERHANGS FND WALL 1/4"

FILTER FABRIC
2-#5's T&B
BASEMENT EL. 91'0"

DRAIN ROCK
2x4 KEY

1'10"

Manor House with Music

Mamaroneck, New York

This private house includes performance space for frequent chamber music concerts and facilities for entertaining on a grand scale. At the same time, it works well for a couple, who, though visited often by children and guests, live alone. From public concerts for one hundred to private dinners for two, the house needs to both be vast and seem intimate, depending on the occasion.

The deep, narrow site faces Long Island Sound, with neighbors on either side. The house is L-shaped, which separates service functions (laundry, service apartment, garages) from living and common areas. The service wing screens the house from its nearest neighbors, while the living wing faces the shore, giving each room a clear view of the open water. The large front courtyard provides a formal approach and visitor parking, its surrounding walls cut with openings for views of the landscape. The courtyard itself is rotated off-axis to produce an asymmetry that softens its formality and modulates the scale of the facade.

The rationalist facade, with windows punched in unbroken rhythm, is relieved of its formal regularity by the strength of the gable ends. Another in the series of pitched-roof houses, this residence uses the roofs as familiar signs, masking the modernism that would be unwelcome in a suburban community.

Landscape elements actively extend the house in both directions: the courtyard makes an exterior public space while the trellised terrace makes the pool a private outside room facing the Sound. The interior is organized as a series of interrelated rooms within a larger volume that includes transition spaces which, like the balconies, offer good viewing and listening areas for the concerts. No single room is oversized—several are quite small, in fact—but when used in combination, accommodate large groups. The master suite functions efficiently as a separate house in itself.

Above: A pool and trellised terraces create a foreground to views of Long Island Sound.

Opposite Page: A continuous wall provides a unifying enclosure to the entrance court. The two-story facade is rotated slightly, reducing its scale and subverting its symmetry.

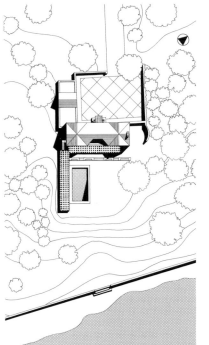

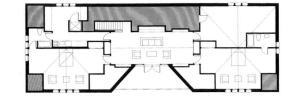

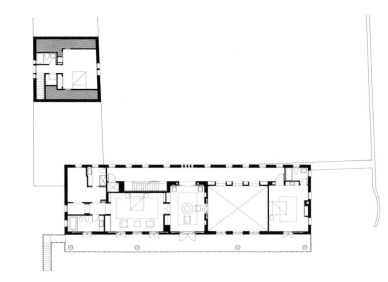

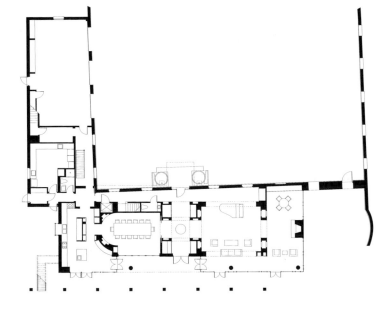

Left: *Every room faces the water, each with access to an outside terrace or deck. The decks are cut into the facade to reduce its scale and to provide protected outdoor space.*

Opposite Page: *A cantilevered concrete stair gives direct access to the pool and grounds from the master bedroom and guest room. The trellis both focuses the view toward the Sound and provides shade for the pool while screening it from the neighbors to the west.*

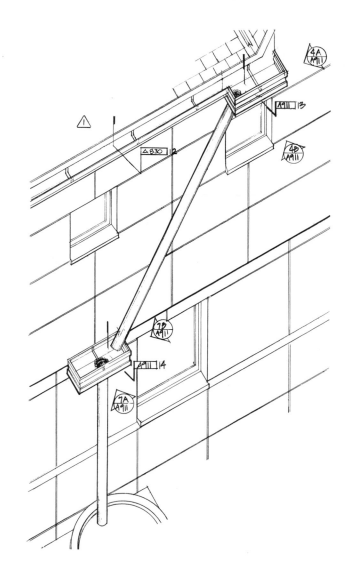

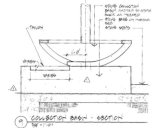

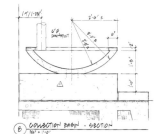

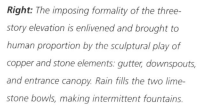

Right: *The imposing formality of the three-story elevation is enlivened and brought to human proportion by the sculptural play of copper and stone elements: gutter, downspouts, and entrance canopy. Rain fills the two lime-stone bowls, making intermittent fountains.*

Opposite Page: *In contrast to a traditional reading of the pitched-roof facade, a strong modernist image is created by the rationalist pattern of square windows and the strong entry figure with its steel canopy, drain spout assemblage, and central gridded window.*

Right: The two-story living room—in plan, a room within a room—doubles as a chamber-music hall. Designed for acoustic quality, it seats one hundred listeners.

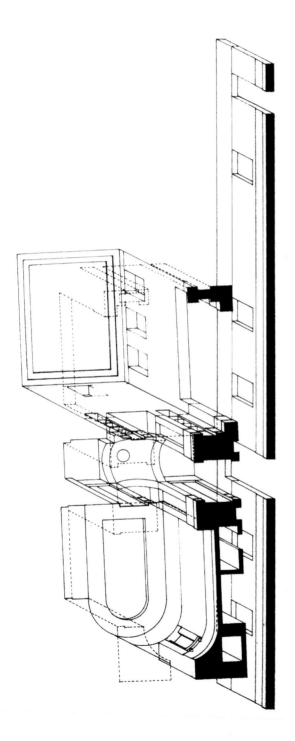

Left: The linear first-floor plan, with its central hall and pendentive arch at the entrance cross-axis, is designed to accommodate large gatherings. The upstairs is private, its major stairway shielded from the public spaces. The intimate family room looks out on the courtyard and down through an oculus to the central hall below.

Two-Sided House

Lincoln, Massachusetts

This house was designed to resolve several conflicts: first, between the conservative tastes of an exurban community and the family's desire for modern forms; second, between the clients' wish for architectural anonymity in the neighborhood and their desire for personal expression in their home; and third, the inclination toward an open, transparent architecture and the need for the warmth and privacy of closed spaces.

The house takes two positions. On the public side, the facade presents a gable and cornice that evoke, but do not reproduce, traditional New England architecture—another pitched roof playing its assigned role. With few windows, the grand roof plane insulates the house from harsh north winds and harbors the expected front door to the house. On the private side, the southern exposure has large expanses of glass, open to the sun and the banks of the Sudbury River, its white facade clearly modernist in form and abstract in expression.

The schizophrenic exterior is joined at the sides, where the enclosing idiom of the traditional meets the openness of the modern. Inside, the house is entirely modern, suffused with light from the windows and skylights, its public spaces open in plan and enclosing an interior garden. The children's bedrooms on the second floor open off a room-sized corridor with bed-sized window seats under the eave of the pitched roof, making a "found space" for play and extra guests. It is a family house, ready to adapt to a variety of uses.

Above: *From the town road, the house appears across the Sudbury River, childlike in simplicity, suggesting the familiar outlines of traditional New England architecture.*

Opposite Page: *From the rear, the house is unabashedly modernist. The south facade, which looks on to an unspoiled pond and bird sanctuary, is almost entirely glass. Second-story bedroom windows have a freestanding screen for awnings, while the overhang of the balcony above shades the first-floor kitchen and study.*

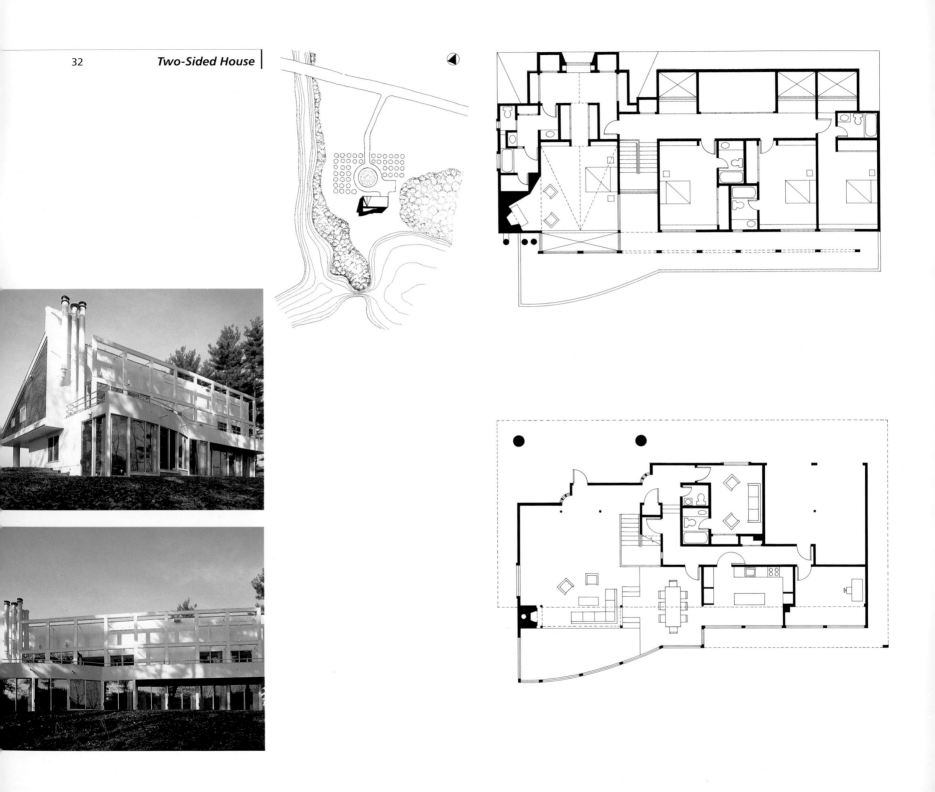

Opposite Page and Left: *Resolution of the two opposing facades occurs on the side elevation, where the pitched-roof forms interlock with the pure orthogonal shapes. From the street, the house evokes vernacular tradition, yet its elements are far from representational: the entrance gable is greatly overscaled, as are its two supporting columns. The entry overhang is equally oversized, hovering with no apparent support. The fireplace mass, upon closer inspection, also appears to float above the pitched roof. The south elevation, by contrast, is stripped of all conventional form.*

Above: *Entering beneath the low, enveloping, superscaled gable, one passes into the living room and confronts a bright, full-height glass wall open to the lawns and pond. An operable skylight provides ventilation for a greenhouse space.*

Right: *Architectural expression within the house is purely abstract and without ornament, save for one residual molding that recalls the 2-foot (61-cm) deep entrance cornice.*

Opposite Page: *A later addition to the house comprises a garage with a separate apartment.*

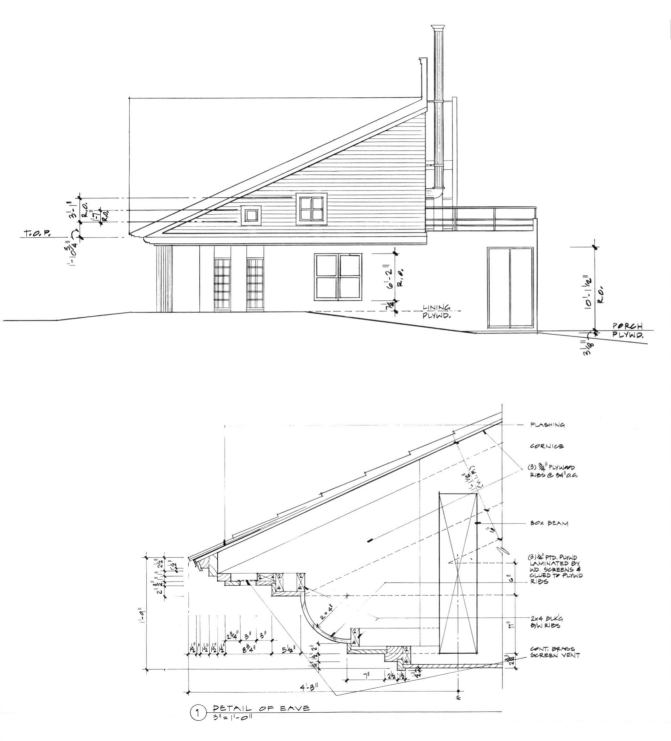

T.O.P.

LINING
PLYWD.

PORCH
PLYWD.

FLASHING

CORNICE

(3) 3/4" PLYWOOD
RIBS @ 34" O.C.

BOX BEAM

(3) 1/4" PTD. PLYWD.
LAMINATED BY
WD. SCREENS &
GLUED TO PLYWD
RIBS

2x4 BLKG.
B/W RIBS

CONT. BRASS
SCREEN VENT

① DETAIL OF EAVE
  3" = 1'-0"

Mies House Pavilions and Second Addition
Weston, Connecticut

Mies van der Rohe designed this private residence in 1955, based on his earlier model for workers' housing. He used window-wall units left over from the construction of his famous Lake Shore Drive Apartments in Chicago. One of only three Mies houses extant in the United States, the Connecticut house was bought in 1981 by a businessman who wanted to expand the very small house for use as a weekend retreat. Five years later, a new owner came back to the architect, requesting a permanent residence for his family. In the first phase, two separate pavilions were built, and in the second, the original Mies house was restored and enlarged.

The idea of "adding to Mies" was daunting. The challenge was to respect this icon of high modernism—by then a historical object—without mimicking the original. With respect to Mies and history, the design had to be contextual; with respect to the new owners, it had to function for their needs better than the original could. The task was to engage modernism as tradition and treat the International Style in a historicist mode.

Left intact as an icon, the original house became part of a composition of buildings, which included two separate but linked pavilions inspired by the plan of Mies' Barcelona Pavilion of 1929. One pavilion contains two guest rooms, a sauna, and a Japanese bath; the other, a large common room, complete with kitchen, for meetings and entertaining. The two are linked by a perforated steel screen that also marks the precinct of the outdoor pool.

The early modernist fascination with Japanese architecture provided another point of reference. Japanese elements are echoed in such details as the raised platform floors and the exterior walls that slide into glass pockets, leaving the rooms completely open to the outdoors. While the Japanese allusions are literal, the materials are high modern glass, steel, and aluminum. Mies, who used glass as a surrogate for walls, might have approved of their elimination altogether, a feat not yet technically available to him.

Above: *The main elevation of the Mies house was restored but left essentially unaltered by the two new additions.*

Opposite Page: *The first addition consists of two separate pavilions: one with guest rooms, sauna, and Japanese bath, the other with a small kitchen and party room. The pavilions are linked by a steel screen fabricated by sculptor Richard Heinrich, which also provides a backdrop for the pool and defines the edge of the site.*

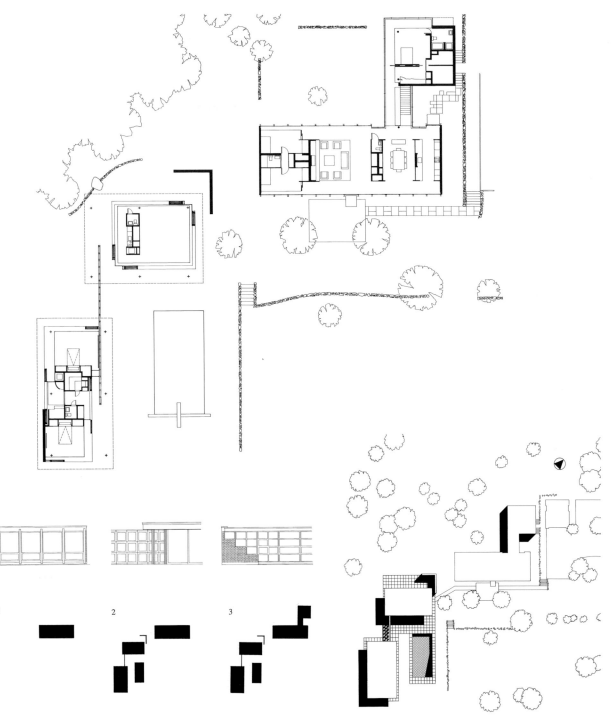

1

2

3

Above and Opposite Page: *Although intentionally set apart from the original house, the pavilions produce a composition that both alludes to Miesian theory and respects the integrity of the Mies house itself (right).*

Below Left: *The pavilions experiment with glass both moving and fixed: sliding glass walls open completely, and the perforated screen is glazed when enclosing a room, and open when out-of-doors.*

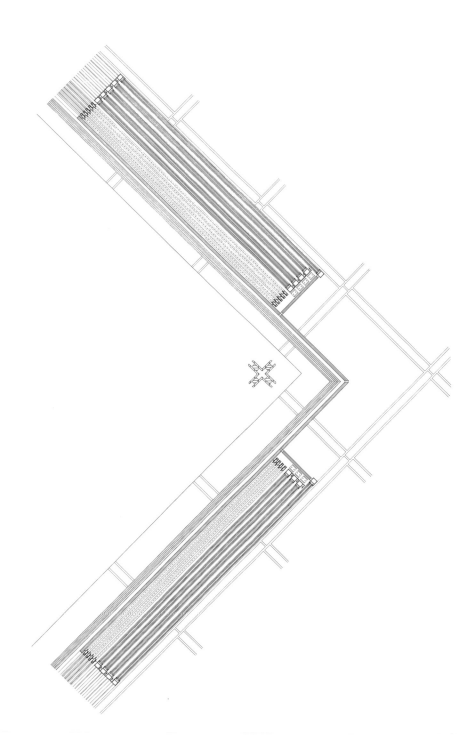

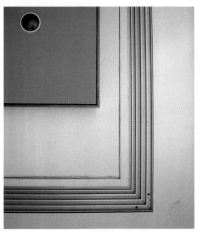

Left and Opposite Page: *The sliding glass panels and screens are stored in glass enclosures at opposite corners of the rooms. The dropped ceiling and raised floor demarcate the living spaces within the open pavilions. Reflections of vertical wall and horizontal roof planes on the glass panels create shifting patterns of opaque and transparent images.*

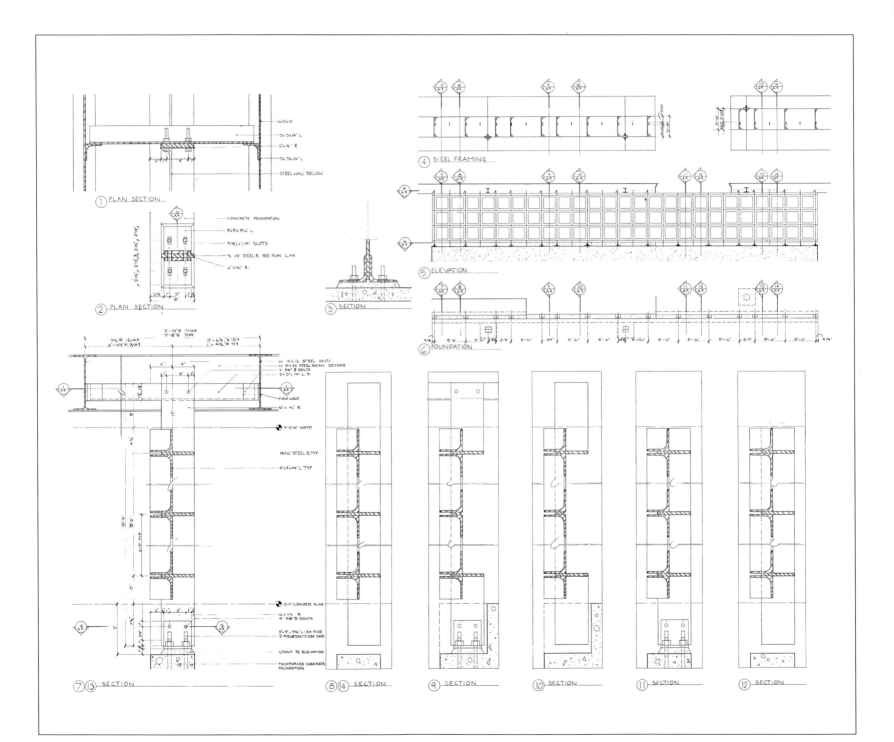

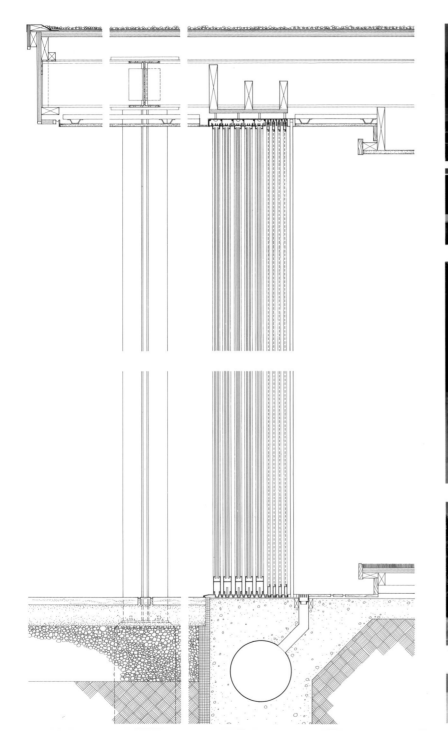

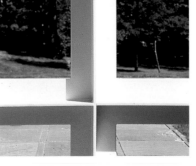

Left: The stone paving patterns, perforated screen wall, and column placement conform to the dimensions of Mies's grid.

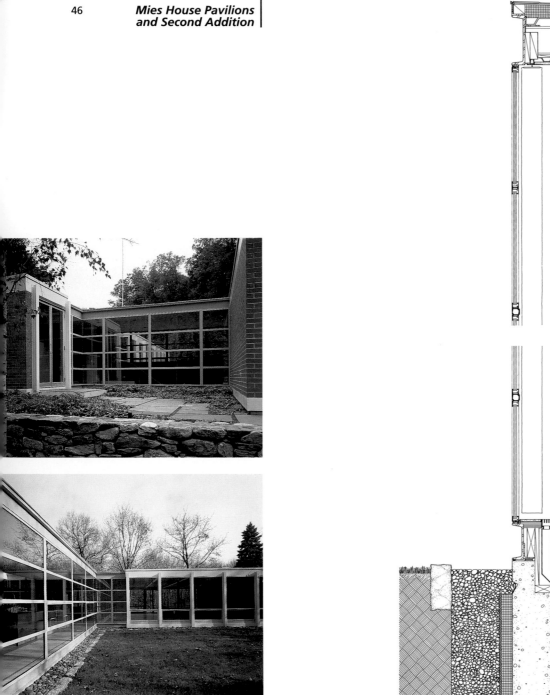

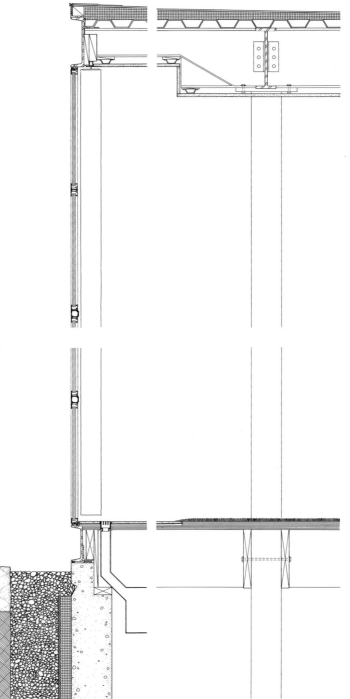

Left: *The second new addition is let into the original structure, replacing four bays of its window wall and inserting one round column for support. The new horizontal glass wall turns the corner and marks the location of the missing Mies columns. All new construction is identified by its horizontal steel window system, which contrasts with the verticality of the original.*

Opposite Page: *The second addition both creates an entrance courtyard and specifies one of Mies's bays as the entrance to the house, which had not been identifiably marked in the original.*

Above: *Accurate restoration of the living room included the replacement of deteriorated wood paneling, installation of the original travertine floor (designed but never laid), and repair of the steel roof system and window walls.*

Right: *The second addition contains a master bedroom, full kitchen, separate dining room, and basement playroom and utilities.*

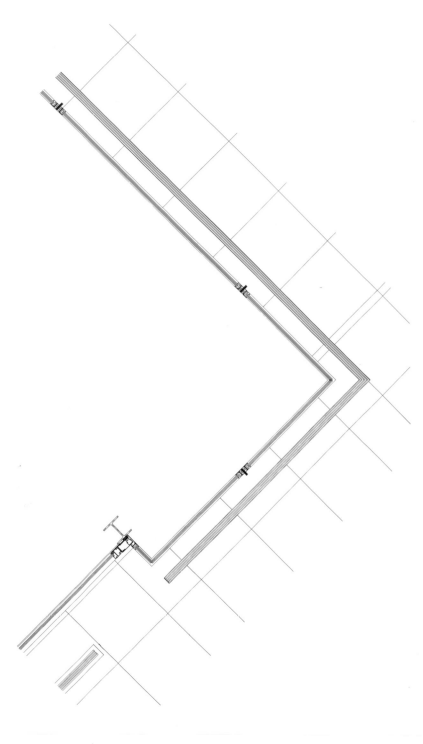

Above and Center Left: Extending Mies's use of glass, the design uses glass as an object itself, here shown at corridor to new bedroom and in new bathroom.

Left: A steel column (detail) supports a free-form maple desk in the study area of the master bedroom suite.

Addition to Usonian House

Pleasantville, New York

L ocated in the "Usonian" community designed by Frank Lloyd Wright, this house was originally built by a disciple of Wright's in 1954 at a cost of less than ten thousand dollars. Compared with three neighboring masterpieces by Wright himself, not only did the house suffer from the somewhat ill-conceived design of an acolyte, but its inexpensive materials had grown worn and shabby over the years. The new owners wanted more space, and the house needed complete rehabilitation.

The task was to correct the building's ungainly aspects and make it work as a much larger family house. The contextual challenge was not so much to preserve the original as it was to improve it: to make the Wrightian elements more Wrightian, the modernist forms stronger, and the connection to the surrounding woodland more direct. Set on a steep, wooded site, the top floor with its carport, open planning, slanted roof, and views of the woods, possessed the best features of Wright's Usonian ideal. But the rest of the original three-story structure was awkward in appearance and provided no access to the outdoors.

The new barrel-shaped addition wraps around the lower two floors, forming a plinth for the top floor, which now reads as a one-story building whose horizontality is highlighted as the most authentic Wrightian element. Partitions were removed and glass added on the top floor to enhance this purity of image. The barrel contains four new bedrooms and two bathrooms, and its roof becomes a terrace under the canopy of forest, providing usable outdoor space where before there was none. The house has an elegant and practical living and dining floor; the bedrooms are on the lower level, with the children's rooms and playroom separated from the master suite. All rooms have a view of the woods.

Above: From the street, the soaring roof, carport, and horizontal cypress siding comprise the typical image of Wright's Usonian House. Here it has been preserved, restored, and enhanced with additional glass in the living spaces. From this perspective, the new addition appears only as a platform on which the Wrightian icon sits.

Opposite Page: Seen from the bottom of the hill, the barrel-shaped addition—forming a plinth for the Wrightian top floor—encircles the two lower levels of the original building and contains four new bedrooms. New horizontal railings in dark red stucco, together with the original roof-plane of the living room, contrast dramatically with the white stucco of the new circular form.

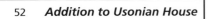

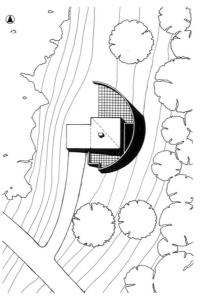

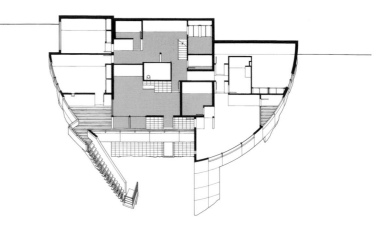

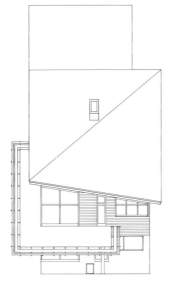

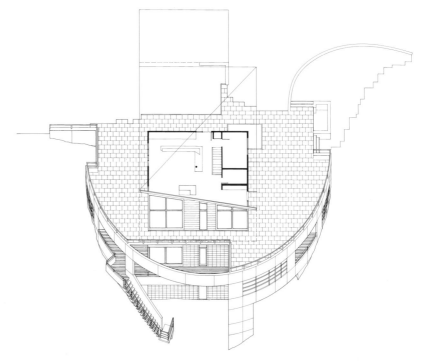

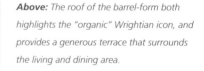

Above: *The roof of the barrel-form both highlights the "organic" Wrightian icon, and provides a generous terrace that surrounds the living and dining area.*

Opposite Page: *Best suited to gently sloping land, the Wrightian design of the original house seemed awkward on this steep-sided site. The three stories not only compromised the house's best feature—the horizontal upper floor—but there was no access to the wooded landscape or to the common lands of Wright's original site plan, which lie at the bottom of the hill.*

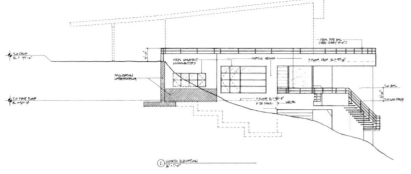

2 NORTH ELEVATION
   ¼" = 1'-0"

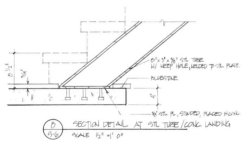

6'-0"

#6 @ 12" O.C.
#6 @ 8" O.C.

#4 @ 12" O.C. BOTH WAYS

4 - #4

TO FTG.
-3'-0" BELOW GRADE

7 SECTION DETAIL AT CONC. LANDING
8-6 SCALE ½" = 1'-0"

6" x 3" x ⅜" STL TUBE
W/ WEEP HOLE, WELDED TO STL PLATE.

BLUESTONE

⅜" STL. PL. STUDDED, PLACED IN CONC.

8 SECTION DETAIL AT STL TUBE / CONC. LANDING
8-6 SCALE ½" = 1'-0"

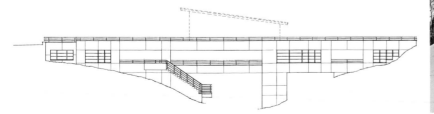

ADDITION ELEVATION (FLATTENED)
SCALE ⅛" = 1'-0"

Left: A gentle stairway wraps around the barrel, descending to a concrete platform, which permits easy access to the woodlands. The new terrace, deck, and stairway all enhance the experience of seasonal change that Wright so often stressed. Here, winter snows alter the feeling of the natural setting and of the interior of the house as well.

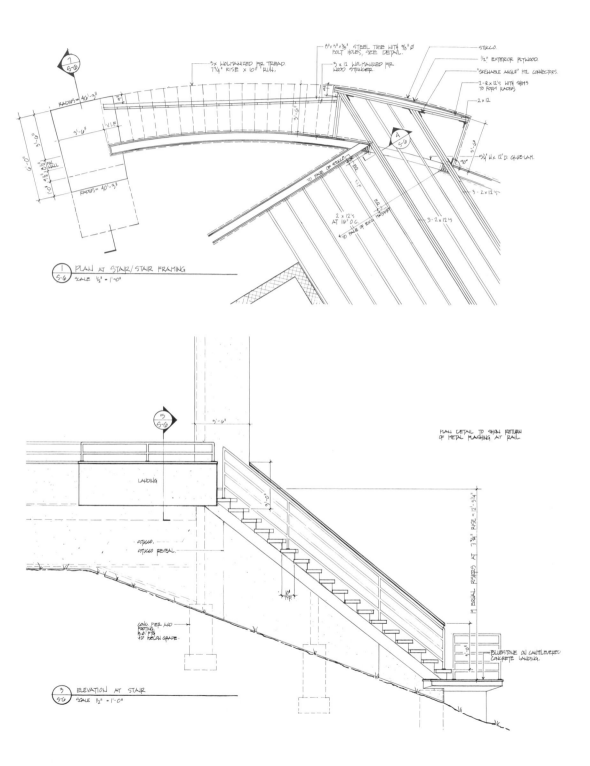

Left: *Sculptural cut-outs reduce the scale of the 85-foot (26-meter) diameter barrel form, and they also frame views of the landscape from inside. From outside, the openings provide glimpses of the horizontality of the original house, while the circular form stands on its own terms, removed from any direct reference to Wright.*

Opposite Page: *Symmetrical steel windows offer horizontal vistas from the bedrooms on the new lower story inside the barrel. Because of the steepness of the site, these lower-level rooms feel as if they are suspended in the midst of the trees.*

Right: Interior modifications included restoring the wood ceilings and the original sculptured concrete-block fireplace. A couch and planter were designed in the Wrightian manner, and a new homogeneous linoleum floor—of the sort favored by Wright—replaced inappropriately added Mexican tile.

Opposite Page, Below: A small terrace is cut out of the barrel, giving the master bedroom its own private exterior space.

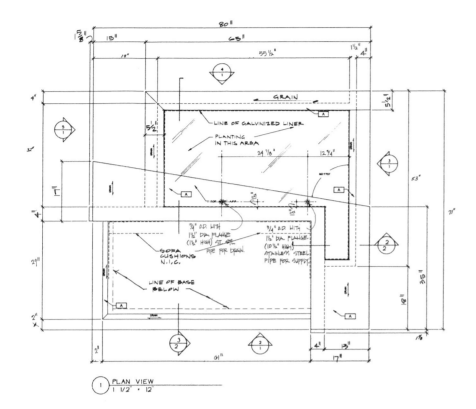

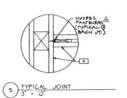

GRAIN

LINE OF GALVINIZED LINER

PLANTING IN THIS AREA

SOFA CUSHIONS N.I.C.

LINE OF BASE BELOW

3/4" O.D. WITH 1 1/2" DIA. FLANGE (1 1/2" HIGH) ST. STL. PIPE FOR DRAIN.

3/4" O.D. WITH 1 1/2" DIA. FLANGE (10 1/2" HIGH) STAINLESS STEEL PIPE FOR SUPPLY.

1 PLAN VIEW
1 1/2" = 12"

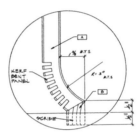

MODEEZ FASTENERS (TYPICAL @ EACH JT.)

5 TYPICAL JOINT
3" = 12"

KERF BENT PANEL

SCRIBE

R = 3" B.T.S

4 FOOT DETAIL
FULL - SEE SKETCH "A"

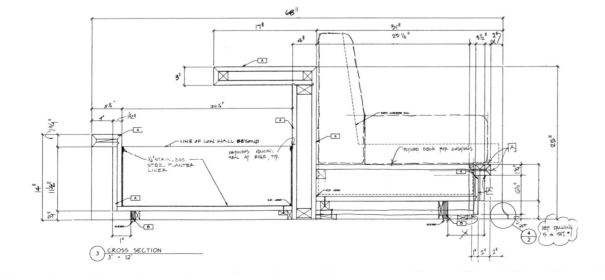

LINE OF LOW WALL BEYOND

1/8" STAINLESS STEEL PLANTER LINER

CONTINUOUS SILICON SEAL AT EDGE, TYP.

SOFA CUSHIONS ALL.

PLYWOOD DECK FOR CUSHIONS

REF. DRAWING 5 IN SHT.

3 CROSS SECTION
3" = 12"

Farmhouse with Lap Pool and Sunken Garden

Worcester, New York

Above: *The original farm buildings and the shapes of the new structure form a modernist composition that also evokes vernacular rural architecture.*

Opposite Page: *The sunken garden on the pool level—directly accessible from the gallery and master bedroom—is cut into the flat plane of the river valley site. Because the view is just below ground level, privacy is assured without the need for walls that would obstruct the open landscape.*

This eighteenth-century white frame farmhouse, situated in an open field with a view of two silos and a hillside beyond, presented a perfect picture of American rural vernacular architecture. The owners asked for an addition that would be twice as large as the original, and would include an art gallery and a lap pool.

The context demanded a design that would sustain multiple readings, allowing the original house to remain prominent in the composition without limiting the sculptural possibilities of the new structures. The new forms evoked the outbuildings traditionally added to the rear of farmhouses, and their shapes and materials linked them to the barns and silos on the site, all in an abstract way consistent with the principles of what the architect calls "contextual modernism." The same design principles developed earlier for the modern masters in the Mies and Wright projects, operate here with an anonymous vernacular building, whose addition enhances the original both by respect and contrast.

Four separate forms contain the new living room, master bedroom suite, the gallery, and the pool, their separateness reducing what might otherwise be the overwhelming size of the new structure. To maintain an appropriate scale between the old and the new, the fifteen-foot high, ninety-five-foot long lap pool building is literally suppressed one level, so that the pool opens on to a sunken garden and terrace, which offers privacy without obstructing the landscape with fences or walls. The buildings both respond to the larger landscape and create landscapes of their own, which extend the house into exterior spaces defined by the combination of built and landscape form. Architecture does not stop at the outer wall of the building but integrally includes the space created by the reshaped earth and the surfaces composed by plantings.

The resulting composition now functions as a family homestead and retirement retreat, as well as a center for the display of local artists' work. The two functions are spatially and symbolically separated, but not remote from one another.

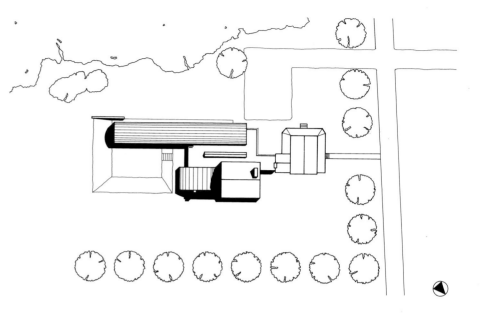

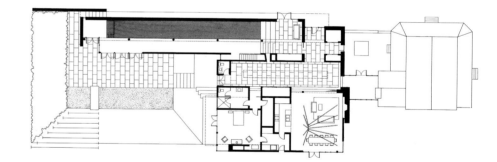

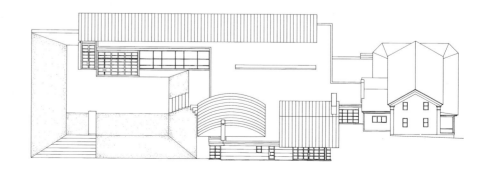

Left: *The additions to the Federal-style farmhouse are conceived as a composition of shapes that both contrast with and complement the eighteenth-century original. There is conscious ambiguity between the impression of multiple vernacular outbuildings and the reading of formal geometries.*

Opposite Page: *Color and texture of material enhance modernist shapes and forms. The pool area combines multicolor Indian slate, ochre stucco, aluminum-leaf ceiling, fieldstone wall, and polished natural-beechwood columns.*

Right: The lap pool creates a transitional space between the main living areas and the sunken exterior garden. In the summer, the steel-and-glass wall opens to make the pool continuous with the outside. The bar and seating area on the upper level integrates the pool space into the more formal rooms of the house.

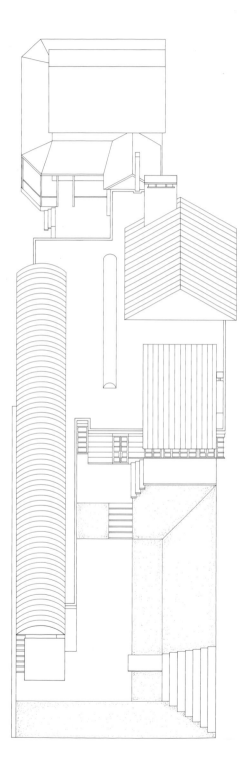

Left: The play of light and shadow through the window walls and the patterns created by the different materials enrich the simple shapes, and they enhance the ambiguity between inside and outside.

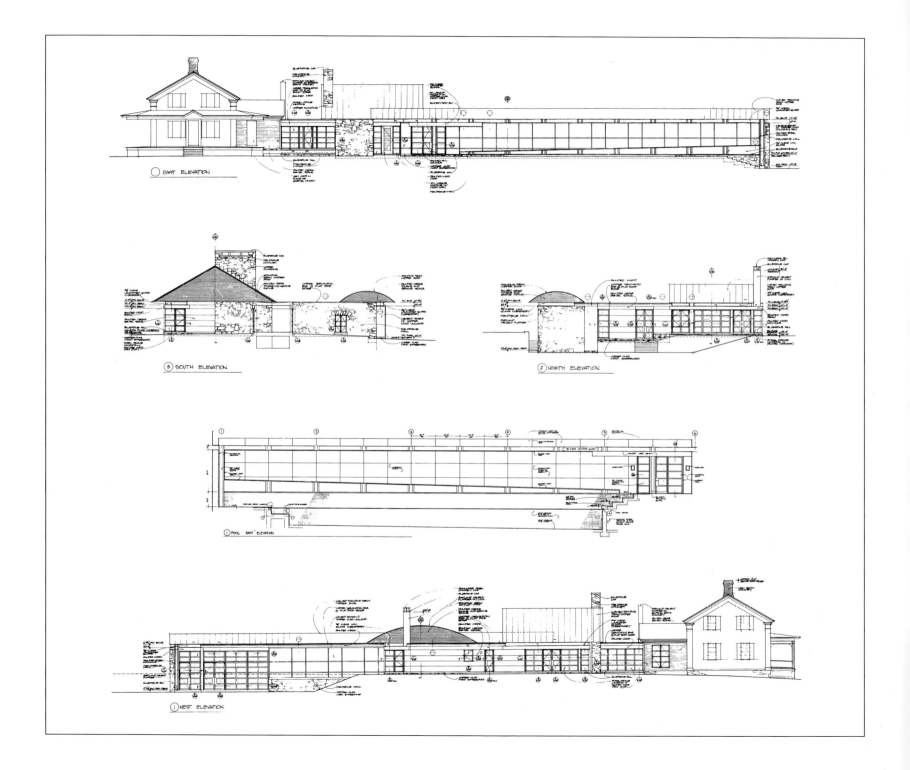

EAST ELEVATION

SOUTH ELEVATION

NORTH ELEVATION

POOL EAST ELEVATION

WEST ELEVATION

Right: *The structural wooden truss supporting the roof gives human scale to a very large space and implies differentiation within this multiuse room. Reflecting their exterior form, the master bedroom, bathroom, and the hall art gallery retain their formal identities.*

Opposite Page: *Conventionally inconsistent materials are used to express a contrast between formality and informality: the formal geometry on the one hand and the informal setting on the other.*

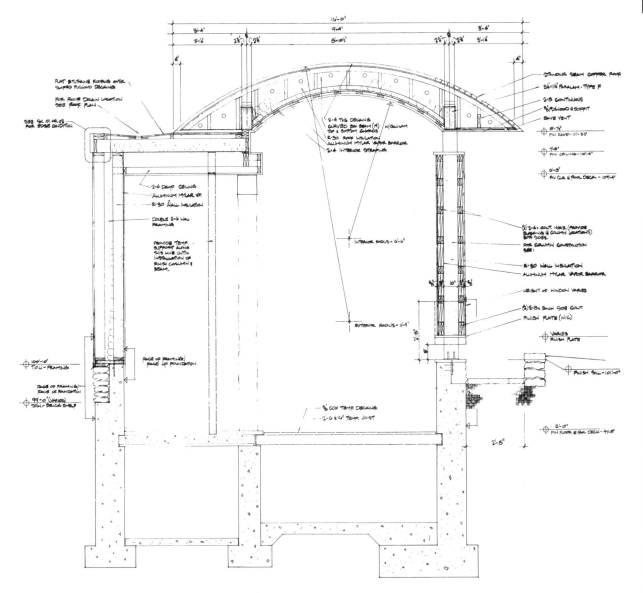

Linear House

Millerton, New York

New England farmers built their houses right on the road, which was their link to markets and to town. They kept domestic activity as close as possible to the house, planting vegetable gardens and raising chickens in the yard, so that the household became a small precinct of order isolated from the spaces of the surrounding countryside. Today, the highway holds little appeal, and the most desirable rural landscape offers privacy, views, and the invitation to wander into it.

To enlarge this early nineteenth-century farmhouse for a family of four with growing children, the relation of house to site was inverted to suit late twentieth-century ideas of nature. The large new addition stretches away from the original house on the road, its eighty-foot extension also making a transition in elevation to bring the house to meet the pond, waterfall, and old apple orchard that had been both invisible and inaccessible before.

The most recent in the series of projects in "contextual modernism," this design confronted two contexts: one of landscape, the other of ordinary vernacular style. The simple, metal shed-roof of the addition echoes the utilitarian aspect of the rural idiom, and the new exterior walkway from the second floor of the old house to the pond and orchard level uses the topography the way local barns once gave easy access to the hayloft.

The addition is a pure linear shape, with two glass facades hung on a rationalist post-and-beam structure. Only one room deep, its formal scheme allows each room to view the waterfall on one side and a newly built rock garden on the other, while the cross-ventilation makes air conditioning unnecessary. The linear plan also maximizes privacy; the new rooms are not contiguous, and the new wing, with two bedrooms, study, and family room, provides separate space for children and guests. A new kitchen connects the common living functions of the old house and the new, both of which are designed to accommodate an informal family lifestyle with lots of action indoors and out.

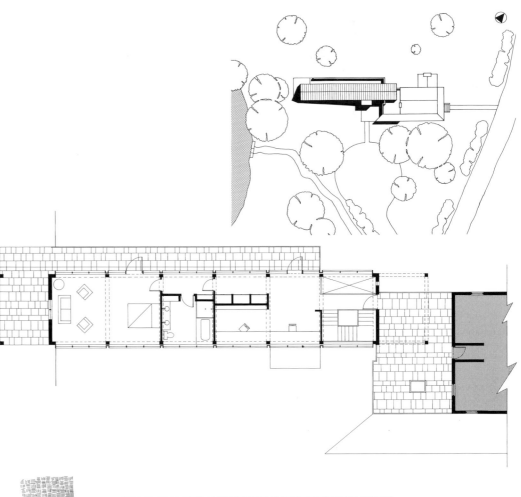

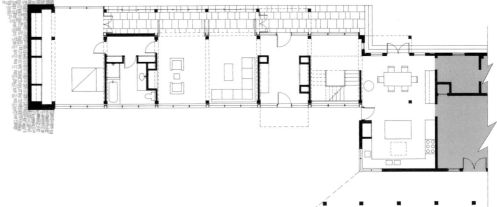

Above: *Viewed from across the field, the bold linearity of the addition contrasts with the ad hoc shapes of the original farmhouse. A single 90-foot-long (27-meter-long) roof encloses the entire new program.*

Left: *The rear elevation expresses the simple, 14-foot-wide (4-meter-wide) plan of the addition.*

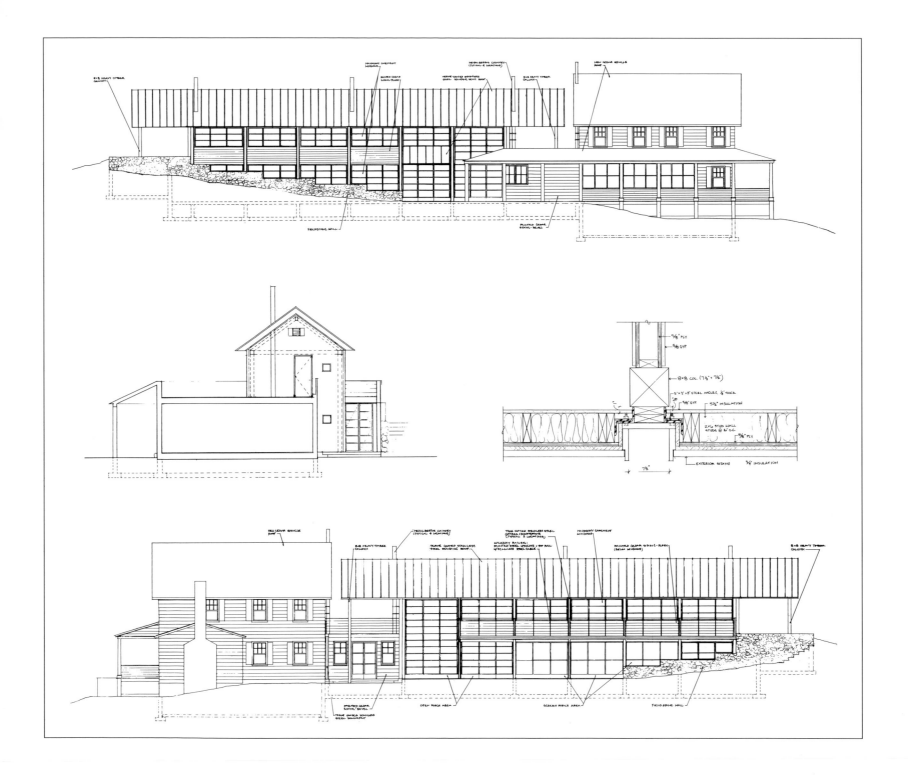

Right: Each room occupies the entire width of the wing and either one or two of eight structural bays. The stair with its bridge to the old house uses one bay of both floors, with the top floor open to the adjacent studio space, and reveals the full height of the building. From the master bedroom there is an unobstructed view of the full length of the building, which reveals its repetitive structural system.

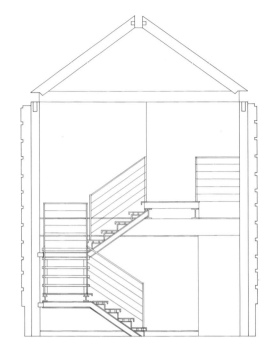

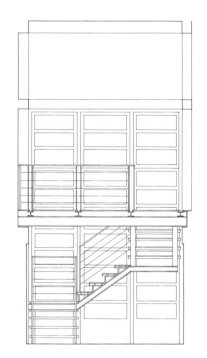

Left: *The structural wood frame and its connections are exposed, making reference both to vernacular rural construction and to rational, modernist expression.*

Bridge House

Olive Bridge, New York

This country retreat for an urban family sought to reconfigure the shape and function of the typical vacation house, which is often just a regular house built somewhere else. Here modernism is neither masked by pitched roofs nor contextualized by multiple readings, but bold and forthright, intended to express in space and form the realities of the building. In this particular case, the site and program demanded bridges both conceptual and physical: bridges between historical forms, styles, and materials, as well as between topographies, uses, and generations.

The house consists of three identifiable forms, each with its own stylistic expression and unique use of materials. The main facade is a large, three-story cube, faced in thin concrete panels akin to cut stone, suggesting the Palladian formality of early American architecture. A clapboard-sided, steeply pitched roof form intersects the cube at an oblique angle, its shape a gesture to regional farmhouses. This form is penetrated by a long, narrow, elevated wing clad in corrugated metal typical of low-cost rural building in the twentieth century. The whole is a composition that evokes three centuries of American rural architecture.

From the roof terrace on top of the cube, a long bridge leads to the bluestone cliffs and connects the formal lawns and rose gardens below and the rocks, waterfalls, and forests beyond. The interior of the house concentrates the common area in the large living room in the cube, places such intermediate spaces as the library, billiard room, and study in the pitched roof form, and segregates the five bedrooms in the linear wing for privacy. Each bedroom faces the corridor, has windows overlooking the woods, and is separated acoustically by an intervening bath. The plan accommodates several generations of family by providing different spaces for different ages and family units, and sleeping space for twenty-four people.

Both interior and exterior spaces are characterized by elements of whimsy and surprise, so that the spatial experience is variable and playful—not so much a house as a place for fun and living in the woods.

Above: A 90-foot (27-meter) bridge leads from a roof terrace to a high ledge of bluestone, ferns, and typical mountain flora. The house itself is a bridge linking this forest environment to the formal gardens and walkways on the rolling lawns below.

Opposite Page: A formal lawn cut through a wooded landscape terminates at a symmetrical cube. The lighted hallway of the bedroom wing pierces an intersecting vertical form, then disappears obliquely off-axis into the woods.

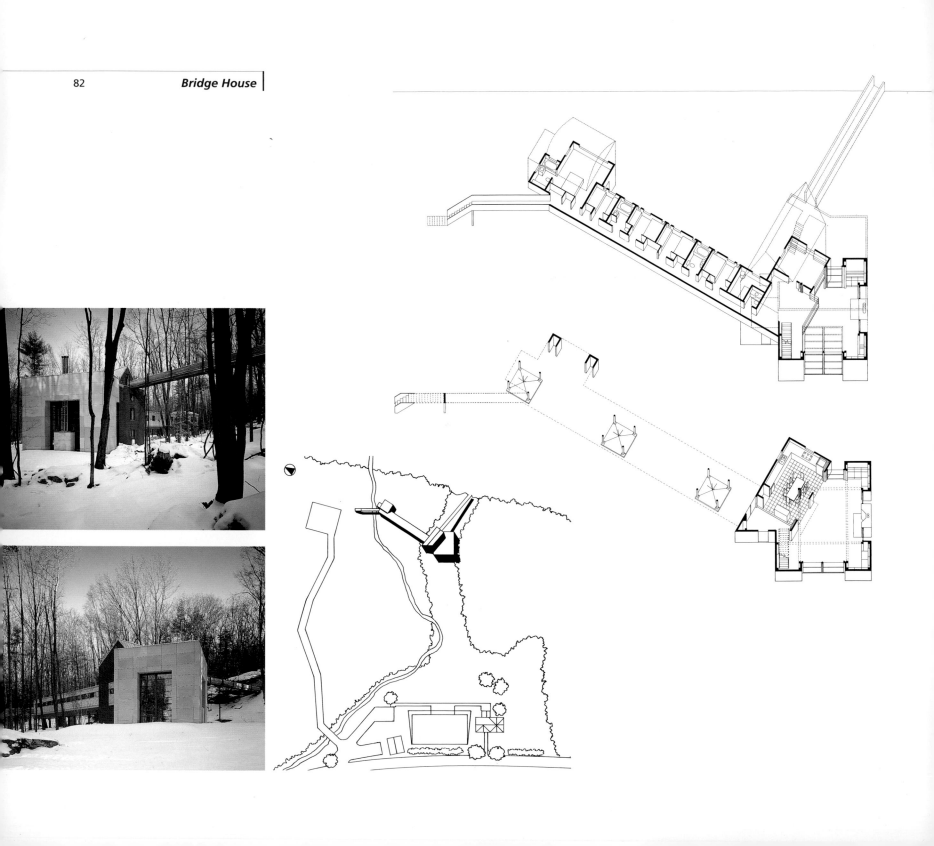

Above: The elevated bedroom wing is raised above the wooded landscape. The high bridge gives direct access from the roof to the ridge with its summer hiking paths and winter cross-country ski trails.

Opposite Page: The three intersecting forms express the program: the concrete-board-clad cube houses the dramatic public living and dining spaces; the 85-foot (26-meter) long metal-faced wing contains the bedrooms; and the three-story pitched-roof encloses the library, billiard room, study, kitchen, and entry hall.

Bridge House

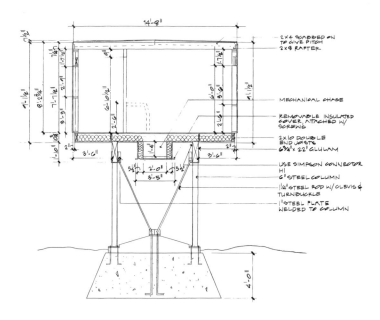

2X4 SCABBED ON TO GIVE PITCH
2X8 RAFTER

14'-8"

MECHANICAL CHASE

REMOVABLE INSULATED COVER, ATTACHED W/ SCREWS

2X10 DOUBLE END JOISTS
6¾" X 22" GLULAM

USE SIMPSON CONNECTOR HI

6" STEEL COLUMN

1¼" STEEL ROD W/ CLEVIS & TURNBUCKLE

1" STEEL PLATE WELDED TO COLUMN

4'-0"

3'-6"   3'-6"

2'-0"

3'-5"

1   ARM SECTION
A13 SCALE 3/8" = 1'-0"

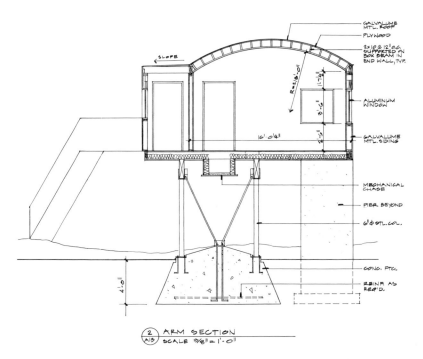

GALVALUME MTL. ROOF

PLYWOOD

2X10 @ 12" O.C. SUPPORTED ON BOX BEAM IN END WALL, TYP.

SLOPE

R=4'-6"

ALUMINUM WINDOW

GALVALUME MTL. SIDING

16'-0"

MECHANICAL CHASE

PIER BEYOND

6"Ø STL. COL.

CONC. FTG.

REINF AS REQ'D.

4'-0"

2   ARM SECTION
A13 SCALE 3/8" = 1'-0"

Opposite Page and Left: *The single-story bed-room wing was designed to make the least impact on the natural landscape while providing the greatest privacy for guests. Insulated from one another by bathrooms and closets, the bed-rooms are cozy, private retreats removed from the social action in the main parts of the house.*

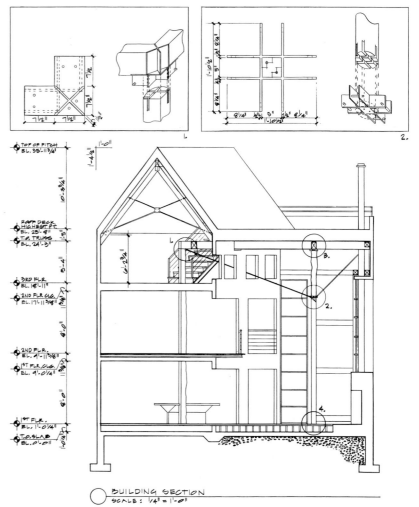

BUILDING SECTION
SCALE: 1/4" = 1'-0"

Right: The seven-foot high fireplace is framed within an 18-foot-high (5-meter-high) window wall. Windows operate as oversized, double-hung units, with lower sections counter-weighted by stacks of bricks. With windows fully raised, the house becomes a pavilion, entirely open to the outdoors.

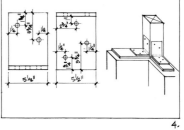

Left: *A series of inverted, king post trusses spans the large living room and supports the bluestone-paved roof terrace above. Steel stairs and balconies lead to the library, billiard room, and bedroom wing on the second floor, to the study on the third floor, and up to the roof terrace and bridge on the fourth level.*

Right: *A large strip window runs the full length of the bedroom corridor, providing cross-ventilation for each room and opening the hallway to views of the woods. One large and four small guest bedrooms each have a desk and work space, bookshelves, drawers, a closet, storage space for luggage, and a bathroom. Built-in double-decker bunks fold down from the wall for extra sleeping accommodations.*

Opposite Page: *The bridge can be seen from most rooms, emphasizing the integration of house and landscape.*

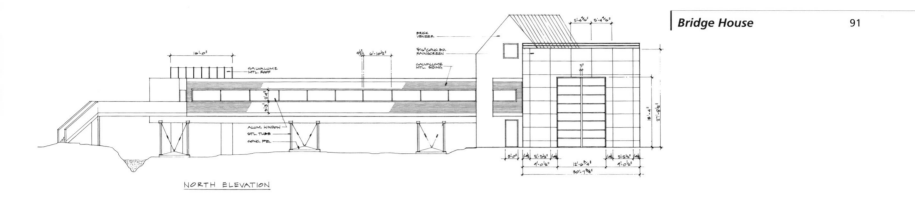

NORTH ELEVATION

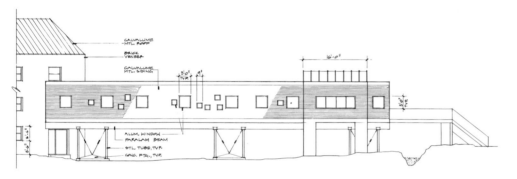

SOUTH ELEVATION

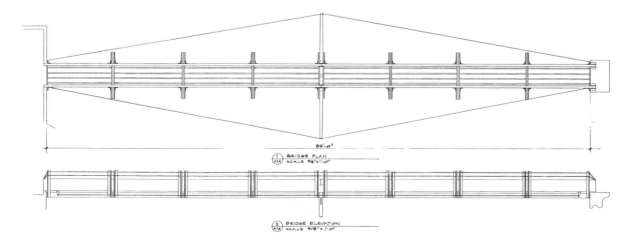

BRIDGE PLAN
SCALE 3/8" = 1'-0"

BRIDGE ELEVATION
SCALE 3/8" = 1'-0"

Lake House with Court

Highland Park, Illinois

Situated on a high bluff overlooking Lake Michigan, this house responds to the beauty and bluster of the lake by creating two worlds within—one oriented to the sunrise, water, and ever-changing views of the Great Lake; the other turned inward toward a courtyard that captures the warmth of the sun and provides a contrast to the often severe lakefront weather.

The strong forms of the house express the two worlds: its curved courtyard facade tears away from the glassed, three-story rectangle facing the lake. The important rooms—living room, dining room, family room, master bedroom, office, and hallways—have exposure to both the courtyard and the lake. A three-foot-thick brick wall curves through the house, a modernist metaphor for the separation of the man-made from the natural landscape.

The house subverts the traditional suburban pattern, which presents the front yard, front facade, and garage to the street. Here, very little of the large house (12,500 square feet/1,125 square meters) is visible to the community. The circular courtyard, separated from the street by a wall, replaces the normal open and unused front yard with a private exterior landscape. The cars enter from the side behind the curved brick wall that contains the garage, directly accessible to the house but out of sight.

The house is designed as a sequence of layers, providing an array of spectacles in which the seasons and the weather are as much a part of the experience as the normal activities of daily life. The plan lends itself to large-scale entertaining and family reunions, and also creates comfortable quarters for a couple living by themselves.

Above: The circular-entry courtyard is faced by the segmented steel windows of the family room. The deep zinc roof overhang provides shelter for the exterior walkway and interior shade from the summer sun. The roof is also an element in the landscape design, focusing sheets of rain, hanging icicles, and piles of snow along the curve of its edge.

Opposite Page: From the residential street, what is in fact a very large house appears in an intentionally low and modest outline. (Photos show house under construction)

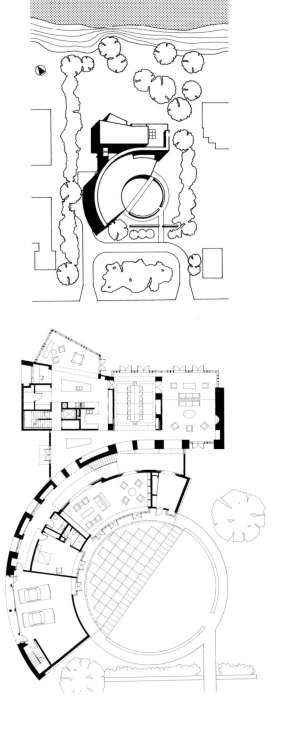

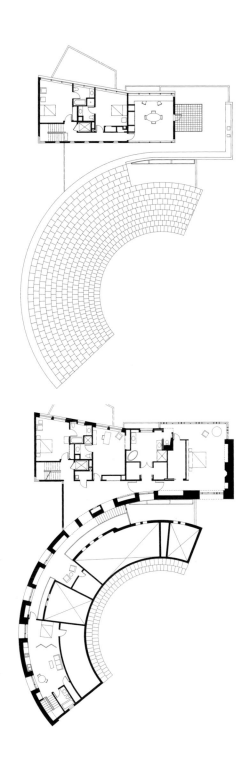

Left: *A two-story glass opening offers a view of Lake Michigan even from the courtyard side, anticipating the dramatic vistas that open up once inside the house.*

Opposite Page: *This early designed model shows the relationship between the circular and orthogonal composition of forms.*

Right: The compound curve of the roof is clad with thirteen rows of specially fabricated zinc shingles. The circular courtyard is crossed by a walkway that separates an abstract checker-board garden of eroded stone and moss from a grass semicircle beyond.

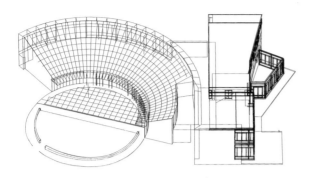

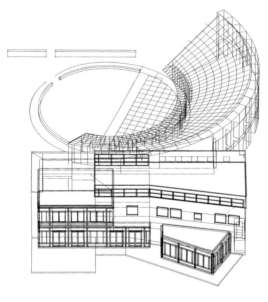

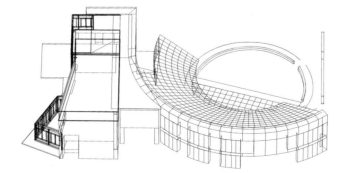

Left: *A three-foot-thick brick wall runs through the house, separating the orthogonal from the circular form and the rooms overlooking the natural setting of the lake from those facing the formal courtyard. As the two shapes split apart, they create an entrance on one side and light for the interior hallway on the other.*

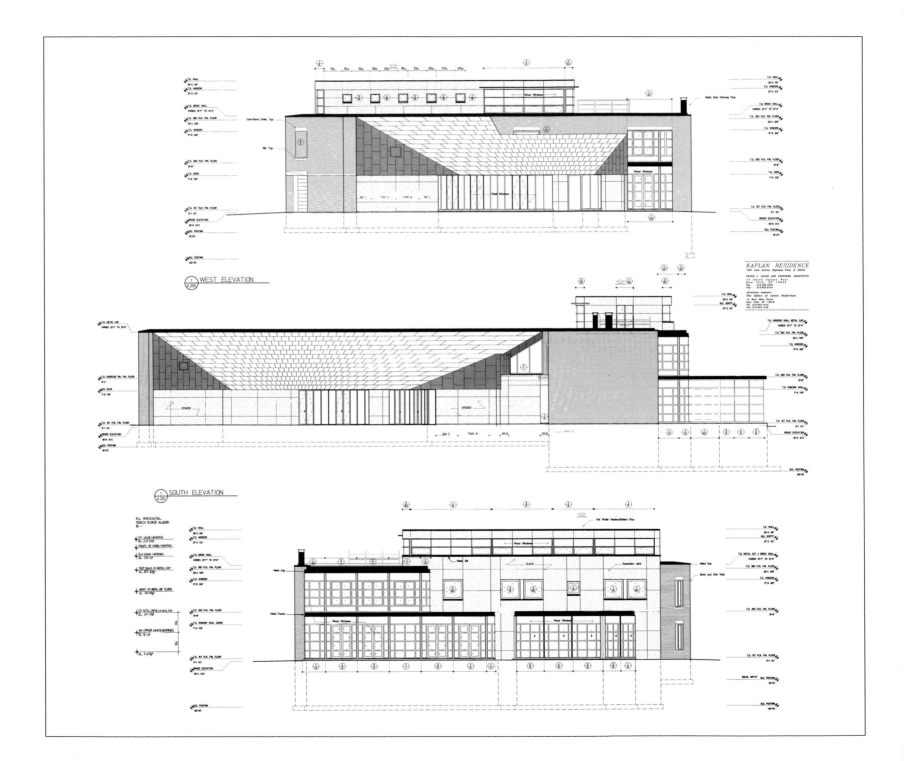

KAPLAN RESIDENCE
1887 Lake Avenue Highland Park, IL 60035

PETER L. GLUCK AND PARTNERS, ARCHITECTS
19 Union Square West
New York, NY 10003
Tel. 212.255.1876
Fax. 212.633.0144

structural engineer
The Office of James Ruderman
15 West 36th Street
New York, NY 10018
Tel. 212.643.1414
Fax 212.643.1425

① WEST ELEVATION
A.200

① SOUTH ELEVATION
A.201

Left: The rear facade incorporates a variety of window types that capture the changing scenery of the lake: a two-story glass curtain wall, linear and square-punched windows, and a projecting glass-enclosed room whose window walls drop below floor level to create an open summer porch.

Urban House

Brooklyn, New York

Building a very big new house in an established urban residential setting requires facing the challenge of introducing a distinctive modern design without destroying the fabric of a neighborhood. Also, the large corner site demands particular attention to the dual public facade the house would show to the street.

Of European origin, this extended family prefers to live urban-style in a close-knit community, yet requires an array of eleven bedrooms and twelve baths. The design is European in allusion, in particular to the early Viennese modernism that stressed simplicity and strength of form.

The form is a three-and-a-half story cube, with its mass broken into three small compositions, almost mini-houses in themselves, which bring the scale of what would otherwise seem an overly-imposing facade into proportion with the surrounding houses. Unlike most corner residential buildings, which have a front on one street and a side on the other, here a coherent sculptural shape turns the corner, terminating each block with equal decisiveness. The third floor at the same corner is cut out to form a terrace enclosed by a trellis and roof garden, with the existing trees along the sidewalk forming a sycamore canopy above.

The rooms are organized around a central stairway and a large skylight, so that light pours in from the middle of the house, allowing the street windows to be shaded for privacy when needed. Because the separation of public from private space is important to the family, the main staircase is screened from the entrance hallways by a two-story open wall of wood and glass. Clean modernist detailing complements a richness of materials, which include mahogany, integrally colored plasters, and stone. The third-floor sunroom, enclosed by steel and glass walls, opens to the terrace, which provides outdoor space—unusual in the city—for gardening, entertaining, and children's play.

Opposite Page and Above: *The cubic mass fills the urban site, but is broken into three parts, both to "turn the corner" and to reduce the scale of a structure much larger than its neighbors. The corner, which faces south, is further articulated by an exterior terrace carved out of the third floor, with a deep trellis at roof-height that implies the completion of the cube. The hundred-year-old trees along the street are incorporated into the design to provide an Arcadian bower shading the elevated private terrace.*

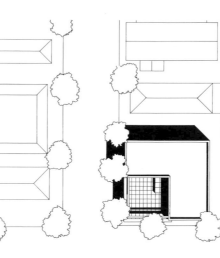

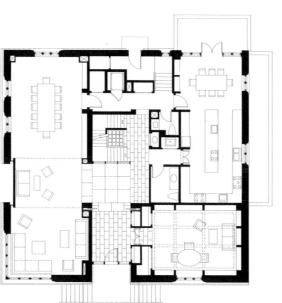

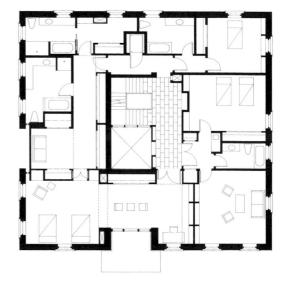

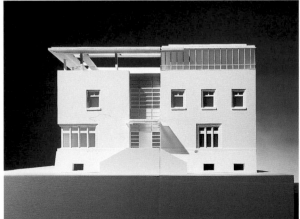

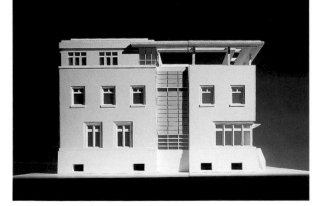

Above: The model cutaway shows the skylit entrance hall and glass-enclosed staircase, which establish the internal organization of the house and provide natural light to the interior of the 60 foot x 55 foot (18 meter x 17 meter) floor plan.

Below Left and Opposite Page: A slightly canted stone base elevates the main living floor above the noise, activity, and disturbances of the street. Large windows simplify the facades of the three parts, which are separated by a recessed curtain-wall of glass and sandblasted, stainless-steel panels.

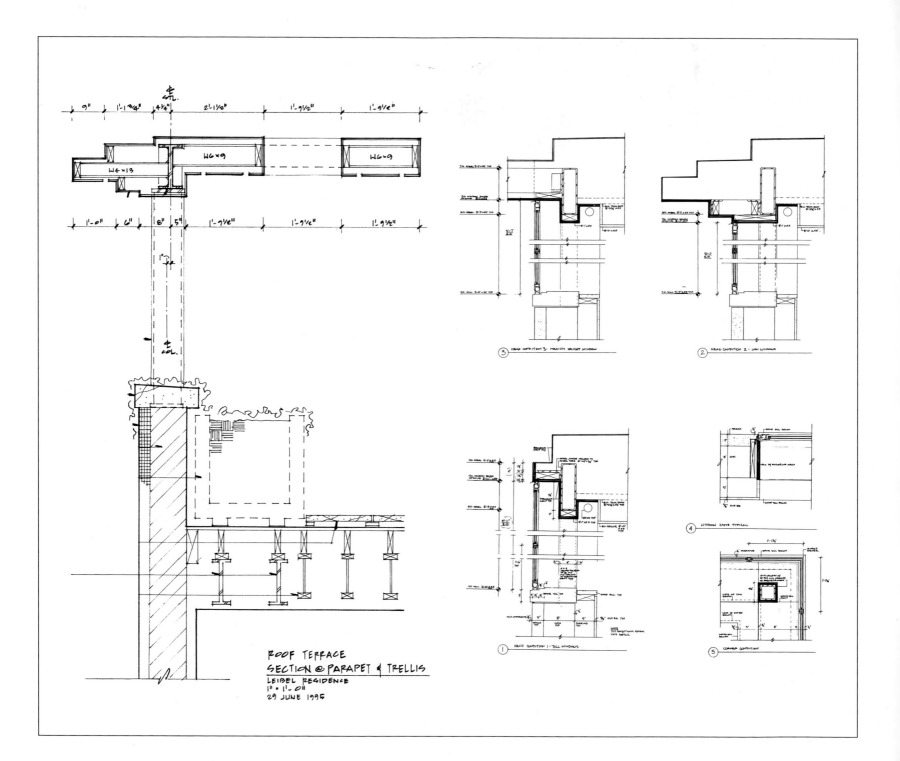

ROOF TERRACE
SECTION @ PARAPET & TRELLIS
LEIBEL RESIDENCE
1" = 1'-0"
29 JUNE 1995

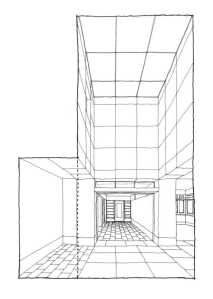

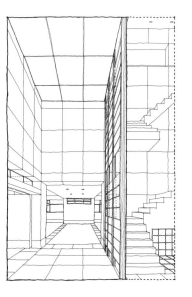

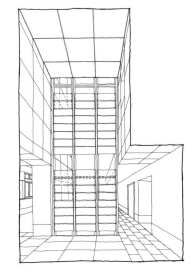

Selected Buildings and Projects

Addition to Usonian House
Pleasantville, New York

Project Staff: Wendy Pautz
Lot Size: 1.25 acres (1 hectare)
Building Size: 3,500 sf (315 m²)
Date of Design: 1992
Construction Completed: 1994

Bridge House
Olive Bridge, New York

Project Staff: Thomas Gluck
Lot Size: 18 acres (7 hectares)
Building Size: 5,800 sf (522 m²)
Date of Design: 1992
Construction Completed: 1996

Three-Gable House
Lakeville, Connecticut

Project Staff: Michael Martin
Lot Size: 2 acres (1 hectare)
Building Size: 4,800 sf (432 m²)
Date of Design: 1985
Construction Completed: 1989

Two-Sided House
Lincoln, Massachusetts

Lot Size: 5.4 acres (2 hectares)
Building Size: 6,500 sf (585 m²)
Date of Design: 1980
Construction Completed: 1982

Farmhouse with Lap Pool and Sunken Garden
Worcester, New York

Project Staff: Fritz Read, Jim Walker
Lot Size: 500 acres (200 hectares)
Building Size: 5,000 sf (450 m²)
Date of Design: 1992
Construction Completed: 1995

Lake House with Court
Highland Park, Illinois

Project Staff: Wendy Pautz, Jim Walker, Fred Wolf
Lot Size: 1.3 acres (1 hectare)
Building Size: 12,800 sf (1,152 m²)
Date of Design: 1993
Under Construction

Manor House with Music
Mamaroneck, New York

Project Staff: Kent Larson—partner,
Cary K. Davis, Mark Hayduk,
Kelvin Ono, Shoji Mitsuda
Lot Size: 4 acres (1 hectare)
Building Size: 11,800 sf (1,062 m²)
Date of Design: 1985
Construction Completed: 1989

Pavilions and Addition to Mies House
Weston, Connecticut

Pavilions
Project Staff: Kent Larson—partner,
Louis Turpin
Lot Size: 5.5 acres (2 hectares)
Building Size: 2,050 sf (184.5 m²)
Date of Design: 1981
Construction Completed: 1986

Addition
Project Staff: Kent Larson—partner,
Cary Davis
Building Size: 1,500 sf
Date of Design: 1985
Construction Completed: 1989

Linear House
Millerton, New York

Project Staff: Suki Dixon
Lot Size: 50 acres (20 hectares)
Building Size: 2,500 sf (225 m²)
Date of Design: 1993
Construction Completed: 1996

Urban House
Brooklyn, New York

Project Staff: Suki Dixon, Craig Graber
Lot Size: 5,853 sf (527 m²)
Building Size: 12,000 sf (1,080 m²)
Date of Design: 1993
Under Construction

Book Presentations Drawings

Elica Manigold

Firm Profile

Peter Gluck received a B.A. from Yale University and a Master of Architecture from the Yale School of Art and Architecture in 1965. After designing a series of houses from New York to Newfoundland, he went to Tokyo to design large projects for a leading Japanese construction consortium. This experience influenced Gluck's later work both in his knowledge of Japan's traditional aesthetics and of its efficient modern methods of integrated construction and design.

Located in New York City since 1972, the practice of Peter L. Gluck and Partners is known for its integrity of design and sensitivity to the relationship between architectural form and architectural context. The firm has designed buildings throughout the United States, ranging in type from hotels, schools, university buildings, and churches to houses, corporate interiors, and historic restorations.

Gluck's belief that the architect must take responsibility for the architectural process from conception to construction has led to his assuming oversight of all aspects of design. The same commitment led him to establish ARCS (Architectural Construction Services), Inc., an integrated system of architectural design and construction management, which provides his clients with sophisticated design, quality construction, and cost management in an increasingly difficult building environment.

Exhibitions of Gluck's award-winning work have been held in the U.S. and Japan. He is widely published around the world and has taught at Columbia and Yale schools of architecture. He has also curated museum exhibitions, including Shinjuku: The Phenomenal City, on Japanese urbanism at the Museum of Modern Art in 1976, and Globalization and Regionalism, which commemorated American schools of architecture at the Milan Triennale of 1996.

Photographic Credits

Henry Bowles

Mies House Pavilions and Second Addition; p. 40 (lower right); p. 41 (top)

Carla Breeze

Farmhouse with Lap Pool and Sunken Garden; p. 69

Jeff Goldberg, ESTO Photo

Manor House with Music; p. 28 (top and left)

Peter Gluck

Urban House (in-progress photos)

David Macleod Joseph

Urban House (model shots)

Norman McGrath

Three-Gable House
Manor House with Music
Two-Sided House
Mies House Pavilions and Second Addition; pp. 7, 36, 38, 39, 40, 42, 43, 45
Addition to Ursonian House

Barry Rustin

Lake House with Court

Paul Warchol

Mies House Pavilions and Second Addition; p. 37, 46–49
Farmhouse with Lap Pool and Sunken Garden
Linear House
Bridge House